Published in the United States by Beaufort Books, Inc.,
New York.

First published in Great Britain 1983 by
Webb and Bower (Publishers) Limited
9 Colleton Crescent, Exeter, Devon EX2 4BY

Conceived and edited by
the E.T. Archive Limited
Chelsea Wharf, 15 Lots Road, London SW10 0QH

Designed by Julian Holland
Picture Research by Anne-Marie Ehrlich
Copyright © Webb and Bower (Publishers) Limited 1983

ISBN 0-8253-0173-4

Phototypeset by Tradespools Limited, Frome, Somerset
Printed and bound in Hong Kong by Mandarin Offset International Limited

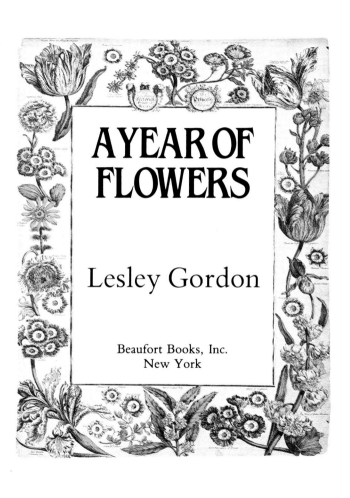

A YEAR OF FLOWERS

Lesley Gordon

Beaufort Books, Inc.
New York

January

Robert Furber, who issued the first illustrated seed catalogue in 1727 under the title *Twelve Months of Flowers*, was a nurseryman of considerable enterprise.

These twelve handsome hand-coloured engravings by H. Fletcher after the paintings of the Flemish artist Pieter Casteels, illustrated for the hopeful gardener the named and numbered flowers that might possibly be expected to bloom in each month of the year, and could certainly be obtained at Furber's nursery in Kensington. The splendid urns in which the flowers are displayed are in the manner of the Dutch masters, and an introductory cartouche containing an artistocratic list of subscribers, including HRH Prince William, Duke of Cumberland, HRH Princess Mary and HRH Princess Louise, gave the catalogue a splendid send-off, the standard of which was perhaps lowered by the publication two years later of Furber's book *The Flower Garden Display'd*, in which the same plates reappeared to provide inspiration for painters and embroiderers as well as gardeners.

The boldest blooms shown in this classical urn are the aloes, the grey aloe and the spotted aloe. But the most attractive of the flowers, the winter aconite, figures in the lower centre. Sir Thomas Hanmer, a devoted Royalist, grew these in the garden at Bettisfield which occupied his enforced leisure during the Commonwealth. In his *Garden Manuscript* he mentions these first among the six plants which 'only Beare flowers in this cold Moneth'.

JANUARY

3

Violet

Gerard wrote in his *Herbal*, 'the double garden violet hath leaves, creeping branches, and roots like the single Violet; differing in that, that this Violet bringeth forth most beautiful sweet double floures.'

Sir Francis Bacon agreed, 'that which above all others, yields the sweetest smell in the Air, is the Violet, especially the White Double Violet, which comes twice a year, about the middle of April, and about Bartholomew-tide.'

Furber's double blue violet is no very great beauty, but perhaps the artist is at fault; certainly he has no means of conveying its perfume.

The violet is an ancient flower of healing as well as beauty. It is one of the four hundred simples used by Hippocrates that is still in use in medicine today. The physical herb women did a thriving trade in London markets selling violet flowers at so much a pint, to eat raw as salad herbs with onion and lettuce, to make such things as sweet-bags, herb pillows and cosmetics, and for use in cooking and wine making.

Syrup of Violets

1lb (450g) fresh violets   1tsp (5ml) lemon juice
2pt (1litre) boiling water

Macerate for 24 hours in a covered bowl, pour off the fluid and strain through fine muslin. Add twice the weight of sugar to make a syrup. Heat without boiling.

Viola canina

February

A splendid scarlet and yellow Duke Vantol tulip is here the first and most outstanding bloom, as is to be expected of the sole aristocrat on this plate. Three anemones tie for second place; the single purple and white anemone, the single dark red anemone and the Prussian blue anemone.

The cornelian cherry or male cornel tree was commonly grown for its fruit, which was made into a conserve for tarts. It was also used in medicine as an astringent and cooler. Furber no doubt included it for its coming so early into flower. If the season is mild the flowers will appear at the beginning of February.

Easily recognizable are the white mezereon and the red mezereon, poisonous shrubs which nevertheless are used in medicine. White mezereon has a yellow berry and red mezereon a red one, and both are poisonous, particularly to children. The plant has many names, including Spurge Laurel and Daphne; the latter alluding to the legend of Daphne's flight from Apollo and her subsequent transformation into the flower that bears her name. A daphne bush is a welcome sight in still winter-bound gardens, but is now rarely found in Britain in the wild.

The blush red dens caninus droops palely above the nearer and therefore larger white dens caninus. Its popular name of dog's tooth violet is misleading, for although its root may resemble a dog's tooth, it lies well beneath the surface of the earth, and the flower bears no resemblance to a violet, but the name has clung to it for centuries.

7

Hepatica

The hepaticas illustrated for this month as garden flowers could, and indeed still can be used for medicinal purposes.

Culpeper says that around 1653, when the first edition of his *Herbal* was published, there were upwards of three hundred different kinds, known to him only as liverworts. He classed them as under the dominion of Jupiter and the sign of Cancer, and says that as well as such unpleasant ailments as tetters, ringworm, running sores and scabs, 'it is an excellent remedy for those whose livers are corrupted by surfeits'—a condition not unknown today.

The leaves of the hepatica are smooth and almost evergreen, with kidney-shaped or liver-shaped lobes, and in the wild state the flowers are generally blue, and more rarely rose or white, but in cultivation variations of these colours may be found.

In American folklore it was believed that sufferers from cross-eyes or a twisted mouth would be cured by a face wash of tea made from the root of *Hepatica acutiloba*, the wild sharp-lobed plant, as well as two teaspoonfuls drunk daily, until the features returned to normal.

Apart from its names of herb trinity, liverleaf and liverweed, it is generally listed as American liverwort. Today an infusion is made from one ounce (25g) to one pint (500ml) of boiling water, for the treatment of liver complaints as well as for sufferers from coughs and diseases of the chest.

HEPATICA *trifolia flore rubro pleno.* *Dicta fil*

March

The calendar for March is rich in anemones.

> That veteran troop that will not for a blast
> Of nipping air, like, cowards, quit the field.

Parkinson said in his *Paradisus*, 1629, that the anemone is 'of its selfe alone almost sufficient to furnish a garden with their flowers for almost half a yeare'. He describes the purple striped anemone as 'tending more to rednesse, whose flowers have many white lines and stripes through the leaves'.

Sir Thomas Hanmer has left us an interesting price list of:

**Anemones bought of Le pere, Oct 22nd 1670
and sent to Bettisfield**

A quarter of an Ounce of Sermonettana cost 1sh.6d.
3 rootes of Felicite cost 1sh.6d.
Halfe of Triumphantes cost 3sh.
3 small rootes of Belle Rosée cost 1sh.6d.

These, and a number more, were 'all set under the South pale in the orchard at Bettisfield Nov.1670', where we hope they flourished, particularly those expensive Triumphantes.

MARCH

11

Auricula

The old name of Bear's ears is somewhat startling until we notice the shape of the auricula's leaves. It was a popular florists' flower, much cared for and fed on rotten sheep's dung of twelve to eighteen months' vintage. Other growers favoured sugar-bakers' scum, goose or pigeons' dung, or dung 'steeped in butchers' blood', for its nurture.

These flowers have played many parts, in humble cottage gardens or on auricula stages. The green-edged, grey-edged selfs, and those with white edges, have all had the honour of appearing upon the stage, and an auricula theatre must have been a highly desirable property. Frequently black velvet was draped over the stage, and the pots of blooms would be arranged in tiers. Mirrors were often placed at the back and sides of the staging, so that these spoilt darlings might be magnified and multiplied. Flowers and leaves become as powdered with farina as the face and arms of a prima donna.

The Royal Widow was one of the most esteemed class of painted ladies, and Furbers says that 'it brings a good truss of well powder'd flowers and is marked with crimson streaked now and then mixt with purple and some yellow here and there intermixed'. A Merry Widow, no doubt.

To the pressed flower artist, the auricula is of particular value—reliable in its sober colours and neat in shape—a good infiller, but as happily taking the centre of the stage.

Moltens Glory of England.

April

With his usual optimism Furber in his April calendar offers his clients a blush-red lily of the valley and white lily of the valley, the latter painted with a most unlikely leaf.

In the past, lily of the valley, *Convallaria majalis*, gladdened the English landscape in May, symbolizing the Return of Happiness in the language of flowers. Today, sadly it is hard to find and slightly sinful to pick in the wild, but at least it remains a plant of no cultural problems in the garden. The whole plant is used in medicine, the root, leaves and flowers being separately dried. It is used as a cardiac tonic, and is a perfectly safe remedy.

The sweet scented ranunculus turns its back and disassociates itself from the floral successes of April. The most handsome member of a large family which includes the buttercup, it takes its name from the Latin, *rana*, a frog, from which shame it seems never to have recovered.

Brought from Persia, Afghanistan and Turkey, the ranunculus become a florists' flower, and by 1829 the English were raising it in many shades. It flourished under such names as Beauté Parfaite and Le Mélange des Beautés, names that presumably were bestowed by their wealthy owners, rather than the gardeners who bred them.

It reached its peak of popularity between 1760 and 1770, but in less than a hundred years its sun was to set. This splendid failure turned its face to the garden wall, and became frog-face, as it was in the beginning.

1 Sceptre Semel Hiacinth.
2 Diamond d.
3 Double Blossom'd Peach.
4 Single Orange Ranunculus.
5 Glory of y' East Auricula.
6 Double Red Piany.
7 Black red Lilly of y' Valley.

4 Brittis King Anemone.
6 Colletadoes Anemone.
7 Amaranthus fruchen.
8 Single Junquill.
12 Iris Minor Auricula.
13 Double painted Lady Auricula.
14 Colerins Church Horm.
18 White Lilly of the Valley.

17 Mirevile de Monde Auricula.
18 Lady Margareta Anemone.
19 Tuliana V.
20 Double Junquill.
21 Duke of Brunford Auricula.
22 Cramp. V.2 Tulip.
23 Albion Elegant Tulip.
24 Brief Tulip.

25 Almond
26 Duke of P. Worst Auricula.
27 Nortis ranunculus.
28 Rentes
29 Double Cucker Flower
30 Elegant Gracens Auricula.
31 Pia Tria.
32 Double flowering Almond.

APRIL

Design'd by M.' Casteels.

Sculpt & by H. Fletcher

Tulip

The tulip, first cultivated in Turkey, arrived in England about 1578. Thomas Hakluyt, nephew of the chronicler, wrote in 1582, 'within these foure yeares there have been brought into England from Vienna in Austria divers kinds of flowers called Tulipas'. By 1620 the Dutch growers had established the tulip cult which led to such speculative hysteria that it rocked the economy of that essentially sober and hard-headed nation and brought it to near disaster. More and more tulips were bred for larger and larger sums until suddenly, in the spring of 1637, the crash came. Everyone wanted to sell, no one to buy.

In England things moved more slowly and less violently. Sir Thomas Hanmer writing in 1659 described 'those single colour'd Tulipes that have rich Blew bottomes stripe often in time with white', and added 'there are little shaking things standing up like little heads of speares within the flowers of Tulipes, which the Latins call stamina'.

The tulip, it seems, has no medical value, although Clusius gave more than a hundred bulbs to an apothecary in Vienna to be preserved in sugar, in the same manner as the roots of the orchis, to ascertain whether they had similar aphrodisiac qualities. They evidently did not. Nevertheless, in times of famine, tulip bulbs have been eaten to quell the pangs of hunger brought about by war.

17

May

The two columbines in this plate, the striped and the virginia may both be lost to us, but the old *Aquilegia vulgaris* and its lovely long-spurred modern hybrids are abundant in our gardens. The columbine is the flower of two birds, the eagle and the dove. *Aquilegia* comes from the Latin, *aquila*, and refers to the inverted tubes at the base of the flower which resemble the curved claws of an eagle. It is called columbine from *columba*, the Latin for dove, because of its likeness to a cluster of doves, with heads pecking in the centre and tails outspread, like the doves of Pliny's vase.

The seeds were in the past used medicinally for measles and smallpox, and with saffron were 'famous against the jaundice'. Doctor Turner, the herbalist, described them as 'looking like flees'. Today the plants are no longer used in medicine, as they have been found to be poisonous to children.

Furber's yellow Austrian rose is *Rosa foetida* or *R. eglantina*, and it is more than likely that his red Austrian rose is that which we now call the copper Austrian briar, *R. foetida var. bicolor*, which was first mentioned by Clusius in 1583. Both roses occur wild in Tibet, and are mentioned by Gerard. The colour in the red Austrian is not quite fixed and it is possible to find both yellow and copper on the same bush, and bi-coloured flowers or even bi-coloured petals. The scent of both roses is heavy and to some people unpleasant, but the single blooms are spectacular.

MAY

19

Iris

Furber shows only one iris this month, the narrow-leaved striped fleur-de-lis. His Persian iris appeared in February and the velvet iris in March. There are two in June, the ultramarine and Prussian blue iris major, and the dwarf striped iris.

The iris, or flower-de-luce, is one of the earliest of cultivated plants, as well as one of the most historic and prolific. It is the yellow water-flag, *I.pseudacorus*, which is generally accepted as the original French fleur-de-lis, since Clovis I, King of the Franks, seeing it growing far out in the river, chose that shallow stretch to use as a ford, to bring his army into safety. The flower was revived as an emblem by Louis VII, and called after him Fleur de Louis, later becoming fleur-de-lis or flower-de-luce.

It has been used medicinally for dropsy and lung complaints, and for a 'pimply or saucie face', and Culpeper says that 'the flaggy kinds [the broad-leaved] thereof have the most physical uses'. The roots were suspended in barrels of beer to prevent it from becoming stale, and in casks of wine to add bouquet.

Orris root is the Florentine iris, *I.florentina*, whose violet scent has been used most extensively in perfumes. It scented the gloves of the Elizabethan court, and a perfume invented by a Roman nobleman, Count Frangipani, was perhaps the most popular of the period.

June

The seven roses that Furber has to offer for the month of roses are of considerable interest. The Maiden's Blush rose has two varieties, the great and the small. They are both albas, with large and spiteful thorns, probably needed since both are beauties and charmingly feminine. They are a pale silvery pink, the blush fading to nearly white, and faintly scented. With their grey-green leaves, these are roses for all time.

Both the blush belgic and the red belgic which is not shown are varieties of damask. These and the frankfort are noted in Mortimer's *Art of Husbandry*, 1721, the latter a supposed hybrid between *R.cinnamonia* and *R.gallica*.

Pieter Casteel's lovely portrait of the moss province rose is perhaps the earliest record of its arrival in England. It stems from the gallica rose, which with provins, centifolia and damask have given us moss roses. The white rose is probably the pale Plantagenet emblem of the Wars of the Roses, that was later united with the red Lancastrian rose, by the marriage of Henry Tudor to Elizabeth Plantagenet, to make the Tudor rose.

The Dutch hundred-leaved rose is the Dutch form of *R.centifolia*. Rosa Mundi has been known for more than eight hundred years by that name. *R.gallica versicolor* was traditionally named after Fair Rosamond, Rosamond de Clifford, the mistress of Henry II who was poisoned by his jealous Queen, Eleanor of Aquitaine.

23

Lily

Furber shows three lilies for June, the double martagon, yellow martagon and the red martagon. Another scarlet martagon figures in July as well as a Virginian scarlet martagon in August.

L. martagon is the oldest lily in the British Isles and the representative of the largest section of the genus. The turks-cap lilies, their popular name owing to the turban-like form of the flower, are listed among the 'herbs for pottage', and for 'Savour and Beaute' in the fifteenth century. A 'Pottys of lylys' was served in the third course of the banquet given after Henry IV's coronation in 1399.

During the reign of Charles I a great variety of turks-caps were grown and they are still occasionally to be found growing wild on chalk hills and in woods in the south-east of England, but one of the loveliest sights to be seen is the fringe of martagons bordering the lakeside at the head of Ullswater. The flowers give off their scent at night.

The uses of these decorative plants in medicine and cosmetics were few, even in the past. When they were used, it was mostly the white lily roots that were pre-scribed for such things as plasters, salves and ointments for the removal of corns. Beans steeped in eggs and wine, it was discovered, when powdered and added to hot water and pulped lily roots, would 'do away the spottys'.

July

Furber's double blue larkspur seems well on the way to becoming a delphinium, if only it could discover the way to be a perennial. The wild larkspur was known as a cornfield weed, especially in Cambridgeshire. The Dutch also cultivated it, but when they doubled it, the spur began to disappear.

The double pomegranate seems to have fallen flat on its face in chagrin, since in spite of its coral-coloured beauty it is unable to compete with the verve of the carnations.

Saving the best until last, look at the lovely white lily striped with purple.

> And this pale nun, who neither spins nor cards,
> ne cares nor frets,
> But to her mother nature all her cares she lets,

Does she not toil like other flowers? Pushing down roots into the dark earth to brace her tall stem against the fretting winds; pushing up the first strong leaves, and finally the sculptured buds; striving to maintain her place over the weeds and over the years, is this not toil?

> O silly lily
> To toil not nor to spin.
> Unless you strive to be a taller, whiter lily,
> Boredom sets in.

JULY

27

Carnation

Furber's flower of the month is evidently the carnation, with its smaller but no less attractive relatives, the pinks and picotées. Both the prince picoté July flower and the princess picoté July flower suffer from unwonted anonymity. Usually royalty thus honoured are named, but perhaps the breeder was bashful. The name of July flower was popularized into gilliflower, and thereafter had to be shared with the stock and the wallflower.

The painted lady carnation stems from ancestry nearly two thousand years old. She herself dates from the late sixteenth century. Although in the early eighteenth century five varieties existed, the original painted lady was almost lost to cultivation, but she lingered on in a few places in England and Ireland.

The painted lady pink was discovered growing in a Monmouthshire garden where her history has gone back for generations. She is single, painted with a delicate pink. The India or China pink was introduced by Thomas Fairchild of Hoxton, the first gardener in England to make experiments in artificial hybridization.

John Evelyn's Recipe for Gilliflower Vinegar *1699*
Gilliflowers infused in Vinegar, and set in the Sun for certaine days, as we do for Rose Vinegar, do make a very pleasant and comfortable Vinegar, good to be used in time of contagious sickness, and very profitable at all times for such as have feeble spirits.

August

Pliny described the hollyhock as 'a rose growing on stalks like a mallow', and how right he was. A useful as well as an ornamental plant, it has a cosy aura of the nursery rhyme still surrounding it. In 1824, Henry Philips, a flower historian, suggested that the hollyhock should be 'planted among the hedges of the countryside, partly to relieve the uniformity of the fields, and partly to extend the honey-gathering season of the bees'. He also said that a good strong cloth could be woven from the fibrous bark of the flower stalks. This was tried in Wales, but no more was heard of the experiment. Perhaps the prospect of looking like a homespun hollyhock did not appeal.

The herbaceous perennial, St John's wort with its shining golden stamens and its invaluable habit of beautifying rough patches of ground when nothing else survives, is a plant of folklore as well as of use to gardeners and herbalists. It was gathered according to ancient custom on the eve of St John's Day, 24 June, to be hung at windows and over doors, or worn as a button-hole, to guard against evil spirits, storms and thunder. For medical purposes, however, it had to be picked on a Friday, in the hour of Jupiter, which is about full moon in July, and worn about the neck for the cure of 'hypochondriacal disorders or melancholy'. Today it has many more practical uses in medicine, including the treatment of children for incontinence, taken in the form of a tea drunk before retiring.

31

Passion flower

Furber's fruit-bearing passion flower has a relative, the three-leaved passion flower which appears the following month. Blooming in late summer, these climbers concentrate their immense vitality in producing flower after flower, even in our damp climate, until frost inevitably lays them low.

To the newly-arrived Spanish settlers in South America in the sixteenth century, these splendidly complicated flowers, then known as Maracoc, must have presented an arresting picture. In their religious zeal the Spaniards saw them as a God-given symbol of Christ's passion—the leaf an emblem of the spear, the five anthers as the five wounds. The tendrils were likened to cords and whips, the column of the ovary to the pillar of the Cross, and the dramatic dark circle of threads become the crown of thorns. So the flower came to be called *Flos Passionis*, changed by Linnaeus to the passion flower.

Passiflora mollissima H. B. K. Bailey

September

The mists of autumn do not descend on Furber's calendar, for the all red amaranthus and the yellow amaranthus will see to that. These are the shattering answer to the poet's dream flower and the sleepy silent fields of Amaranth may after all turn out to be a field of pot-herbs, as some species have done. The old names splintered off by botanical classification have lost us Floramor and Flower-Gentle, and replaced these beauties with such offerings as *A. hypo-chondriacus*, but at least they have allowed us to keep Amaranth, a poet's name, until botanical practice changes, or this strange flower becomes extinct.

Furber shows us in red sow bread and white sow bread two familiar and much loved flowers. It was William Turner, known as the Father of Botany, who launched this delicate flower under the name of sowbread, chosen because the root appeared to be the principal food of wild boars. Cyclamen, made into little cakes is reported by Gerard to be a 'good amorous medicine to make one in love, if it be inwardly taken'.

The little wild heart's-ease was dedicated by old writers to the Trinity because of its three colours, and therefore is to be found in many ancient herbals as *Herba Trinitas*.

SEPTEMBER

35

Gentian

Furber's gentianella takes almost the centre of the picture, although surrounded by larger and perhaps more beautiful flowers. The gentians are an extensive group of about one hundred species and several colours, only six varieties of which are in Great Britain, but the name instantly brings to mind the most brilliantly blue flower in existence. It was supposed to have been discovered and used by the alcoholic King Gentius of Illyria in about 170 BC, but it is now known that Pythagorus, in the sixth century BC, invented an antidote to poison in which he mixed orris root, ginger and black poppy, with gentian and honey.

Before the introduction of hops, gentian root was occasionally used in brewing and in the eighteenth century gentian wine was drunk as an aperitif. As the whole plant is exceedingly bitter, it is commonly used in tonics.

Brooke's Compound Wine of Gentian *c.*1800
Take of Gentian root, half an ounce
Chinchona bark, one ounce
Seville orange peel, dried two drachms
canella alba, one drachm
diluted alcohol, four ounces
Spanish white wine, two pounds and a half

First pour the distilled alcohol on the root and bark, sliced and bruised, and, after twenty-four hours, add the wine; then macerate for seven days and strain.

Gentiane sans tige.　　　　　Gentiana acaulis.

P.J. Redouté   Langlois

October

The single blue periwinkle is a gentle plant whose leaves, 'if eaten by man and wife together, cause love between them'. If that is to be believed, then we should also know that it was once a valued simple for restoring milk to the breasts of nurses. Chaucer called it the 'fresh pervynke rich of hew'. Red, white, blue, purple, double as well as striped, were all to be found—no wonder they were known to the Elizabethans as Joy of the Ground. Although a modest flower, it is a herbalists' plant, still in use today. Beverley Nichols recommends it as good ground cover, and suggests that we all become periwinklists without delay.

Saffron flower is perhaps the most remarkable of the complex family of crocus. *C. sativus* has been used as a medicine, a flavouring, a disinfectant and a dye; it has given its name to a town, and shows in receipt thereof, three images of itself in the arms of Saffron Walden. It has lived adventurously, so they say, travelling as contraband in a hollowed staff carried by a palmer, and it covered in its thousands the flat meadows of Essex, where its stigmas stained the fingers of the women who harvested them for little gain. Also, and this is not the least of its virtues, 'it maketh the English sprightly'. Now it has retired, like a well-to-do country gentleman, into neat gardens in the well-kept suburbs, and perfers not to be disturbed.

OCTOBER

39

Honeysuckle

The evergreen honeysuckle appears this month with the long blowing honeysuckle which was seen in August and which was the most popular among the London nurserymen for its extended period of flowering. It was given the botanical name of *Lonicera* by Linnaeus, in honour of Adam Lonicer, a sixteenth-century German botanist.

Country folk used the juice of its leaves as a mouthwash, as well as to relieve the pain of bee-stings, and to anoint their beehives so that 'the been shalt not goo away'. Its tough stems that follow the sun from east to west in their windings, were used to bind brooms. People called it woodbind or woodbine from this twining habit, as well as ladies' fingers, suckling, and sometimes caprifoly, meaning goat leaf, from a belief that the leaves were the favourite food of goats.

An extract from an unsigned manuscript advises 'Woodbine seed drunk' as 'serving against the Hickop', and it is a comfort to learn that 'an elegant water may be distilled from these flowers, which has been recommended for nervous headaches'. Culpeper extols its value as a cure for asthma and as an ointment, 'it will clear the skin of morphew, freckles, and sunburning, or whatever else discolours it, and then the maids will love it'.

Good Lord, how sweetly smells the honeysuckle
In the hush'd night, as if the world were one
Of utter peace, and love, and gentleness.

November

It is believed that the red valerian, *Valeriana officinalis*, is a true native. What is certain is that the wild valerian is a plant of some education, preferring to grow where medicine and medicinal plants were studied, flourishing on the dry walls of colleges and monastic buildings. Merton College, Oxford, for instance, was once its host, or should we say Alma Mater, and Ely Minster, and the walls of the episcopal palace at Chichester, offered it home and shelter.

Furber displays the broad-leaved red valerian blooming in November, as optimistically as the maiden who

>   in a morn betide
> Went forth when May was in her prime
> To get sweet Cetywall

for both nurseryman and Maiden have extended by two months an already long blooming period. Cats are known to grow as ecstatic at the perfume of valerian as they do about catmint; while human appreciation of the scent of valerian has led to its being given the ancient name of Phu. Valerian is cultivated in England, as well as in Holland and the USA, since the wild plants are not plentiful enough to supply all the demands. It yields a drug which allays pain and promotes sleep, and its use as an antispasmodic is listed in the British Pharmacopoeia.

Peering neatly over the edge of this ornate vase, we see the charming borage with its star-shaped blue flower. Although it is used in medicine, it is most appreciated for its decorative value in sweets, salads and drinks.

NOVEMBER

43

Nasturtium

When Dr Monardes wrote the *Joyful Newes out of the New Found Worlde* in the sixteenth century, he introduced for the first time two important plants—tobacco and nasturtium. Far too much has since been written about the iniquitous tobacco plant, but the blameless nasturtium also has its tale to tell. Casteel's double nasturtium and single nasturtium shown in October, prove that considerable changes have taken place in their appearance since these pictures were drawn. They have also had trouble with their nomenclature, having arrived in England as indian cress, and been given the Latin name of *Nasturtium*, the combination of the two becoming 'the Indian Nose-Twister'.

Parkinson called it yellow lark's heels, in reference to its spur, and thought the flower 'of so much beauty and sweetnesse withall, that my Garden of delight cannot bee unfurnished of it'.

Linked with watercress, *Nasturtium officinalis*, another plant of a peppery disposition, this nose-twister found itself banished to the kitchen garden, as a supplier to 'sallets' rather than beauty. Linnaeus has legitimized the nasturtiums by called them *Tropaeolum*, because the round leaf suggests shield and the flower a helmet, and they thus may be accepted in any garden as *T.majus* and *T.minus*.

Under whatever name it is grown, be it golden gleam or scarlet gleam or mere nasturtium, it can be relied upon, not only to add a pleasant peppery flavour to a 'sallet', but to 'adornate the gardens', as Monardes promised it would.

Tropæolum majus

Capucine ordinaire

P. J. Redouté

45

December

Furber must have depended on the greenhouse for quite a number of the plants he shows in his December arrangement. His scarlet geranium and the striped leaved geranium are not, of course, geraniums, but pelargoniums. The two main ancestors of the 'geraniums' today, *P. inquinans* and *P. zonale*, were introduced in the reign of Queen Anne. When the genus was divided into three in 1787 the wild blue crane's-bill retained the name of geranium, the pink and red African species became pelargonium or stork's-bill, and the small alpine erodiums, heron's-bill. The scented leaves of *P. roseum* and *P. capitatum* are used in medicine, and dried for pot-pourri.

Furber seems well aware of the value of *Laurustinus* in winter gardens and the indoor vase. In November he shows the earliest flowering laurustinus, and here the shining leaved laurustinus. This attractive shrub grows wild in Spain, Portugal and many parts of Southern Europe. It is not known when it reached England, but Gerard mentions it as flourishing in his garden in Holborn in 1596, and Sir Thomas Hanmer describes it in 1659 just as we know it today. 'It is a kind of wild Bay, but with lesser and more crumpled leaves. The flowers are white, with a little red at first blowing about the edges, very small and sweet, and grow many together, after which come some blew berries with a few seeds in them, like the kernels of grapes.'

47

Christmas Rose

Furber's Christmas flower is the Christmas rose. According to legend, it was once called Malampodium after Melampus, a physician who, a thousand years BC, used it to cure the mad daughters of Proteus, King of Argos, whereby the plant acquired a reputation as a cure for insanity.

Around 1663, hellebore was believed to be a plant of ill omen. But then, by contrast, it was given the name of Christ herbe. In an old Nativity play, a shepherd girl, Madelon, present at the Holy Birth, wept because she had no gift for the Child. Gabriel, sent down to ask why she was sad, when told, touched the earth with his staff and up sprang the Christmas rose.

Sources and Acknowledgements

5. Violet, William Curtis, *Flora Londinensis*, 1826
9. Hepatica, G.C. Oeder, *Flora Danica*, 1853
13. Auricula, watercolour by Georg Ehret (Victoria and Albert Museum)
17. Tulips, William Curtis, *Beauties of Flora*, 1820
21. Iris, watercolour by J. Walther c.1650 showing dalmatica, florentina, violacea variegata (Victoria and Albert Museum)
25. Lily, watercolour by J. Walther c.1650 showing martagons (Victoria and Albert Museum)
29. Carnation, watercolour by Georg Ehret c.1750 showing red and white or bizarre violet (Victoria and Albert Museum)
33. Passionflower, Villardel, *Bot. Mag. Madrid*
37. Gentian, Pierre-Joseph Redouté, *Choix des Plus Belles Fleurs*, 1827–33
41. Honeysuckle, M. and J. Fitch, *Bot. Mag.* 8585
45. Nasturtium, Pierre-Joseph Redouté, *Choix des Plus Belles Fleurs*, 1827–33
48. Christmas rose, watercolour by Georg Ehret c.1750 (Victoria and Albert Museum)

Title page: Robert Furber's list of subscribers to his catalogue

The plates of the Furber catalogue were taken from a bound edition dated 1730 in the Victoria and Albert Museum.

The photographs were taken by Eileen Tweedy.

The publishers would like to acknowledge the help of the staff of the library of the Royal Botanic Gardens, Kew.